FANTASTIC SCIENCE-FICTION ART

1926-1954

EDITED WITH AN INTRODUCTION BY LESTER DEL REY

F A N T

SCIENCE-

1926 - 1954

A S T I C

FICTION ART

EDITED WITH AN INTRODUCTIUN BY **LESTER DEL REY**

BALLANTINE BOOKS, NEW YORK

SBN 345-24731-0-595

The editor wishes to thank Edward Wood for supplying the magazines for reproduction. He is also grateful to the publishers and artists for permission to reproduce the covers: The Condé Nast Publications, Inc.; Popular Library Inc.; Ultimate Publishing Co. Inc.; H. R. Van Dongen; and Frank Kelly Freas. And particular thanks are due Ian Summers, who gave freely of his time and help in selecting the best of many covers.

First Printing: September, 1975
Printed in the United States of America
Design by Karin Batten & Elliot Kreloff

BALLANTINE BOOKS
A Division of Random House, Inc.
201 East 50th Street, New York, N.Y. 10022
Simultaneously published by
Ballantine Books, Ltd., Toronto, Canada

THE ART OF SCIENCE FICTION

FROM FRANK R. PAUL TO FRANK KELLY FREAS

Back in the early days, when science fiction was an orphan, there were numerous fiction magazines on the newsstands, representing almost every category of storytelling. There were westerns, detectives, confessions, love stories, family slicks; and there were even magazines devoted to such highly specialized subcategories as baseball fiction, submarine stories, and terror tales. All of these were somehow descendants of other, earlier fiction magazines, and their cover art showed that they were derivative.

But science fiction did not emerge from the same sources as other category fiction. It came from magazines that were devoted to facts and to the technical knowledge of the time. So we might say it derived from the description of a gadget crossed with an explanation of some development of science—usually that new science, electronics.

Hugo Gernsback is generally recognized as the founder and foremost promoter of science fiction. He began publishing it in his early technical magazines: *Modern Electrics, Electrical Experimenter,* and *Science and Invention*. Gernsback himself wrote and published a serial novel entitled *Ralph 124 C 41+* in 1911; the story was clumsy and rather silly as fiction, but it was an outstanding piece of prophecy. The engineers and hobbyists who were the readers of the magazine were enthusiastic and demanded more such stories, and Gernsback happily complied.

In 1926, he went even further by launching *Amazing Stories*, a new magazine devoted entirely to this type of literature, which was then named scientifiction. The motto of the magazine showed its technical and prophetic intent: "Extravagant fiction today . . . Cold fact tomorrow!" Gernsback knew very little about editing a magazine of fiction; but he knew what his gadget-loving readers wanted, and the magazine was an instant success.

By today's standards, the fiction in the early issues of that magazine is appallingly bad, except for reprints from the novels of Wells, Verne, Burroughs, and others. The characters were cardboard at best, the dialogue incredibly stilted, and the plotting was of the most elementary kind. Repeatedly, the story would be interrupted for lengthy explanations of the science behind it. There were mad scientists with beautiful daughters who must be saved, invasions by giant insects, evil villains, and most of the cliché situations that were later picked up by all those bad movies that called themselves science fiction.

None of that seemed to matter. The importance of the stories lay in the wonders of science and of the future. Atomic power was exploited; men went to the moon and the planets; wonderful inventions solved all mankind's problems; technology ruled the world. This was believable then, because nobody had ever really considered pollution, energy crises, radiation poisoning, or any of the distressing later by-products of technology. In the quarter century before the magazine first appeared, men had accomplished wonder piled upon wonder, and there seemed to be no limit to what was still to come. Even the first few years of the Depression did not really squelch that enthusiam.

The magazine's covers reflected the interests of Gernsback and the readers. Whereas other fiction magazines of the time showed noble heroes and beauteous damsels (usually in distress), *Amazing Stories* and the magazines that followed depicted the wonderful world of the machine.

The source of that art, like the stories themselves, lay back in the old science and gadget magazines Gernsback had published for hobbyists and engineers.

Frank R. Paul had been the cover artist for Gernsback's *Electrical Experimenter* and *Science and Invention*. A highly gifted renderer of the possible development of any invention, he was capable of taking a raw idea and turning it into a picture fantasy that was yet faithful in every detail to the original design. With that background, Paul found no difficulty in taking the clumsy descriptions of gadgets found in the stories and developing them into something far more impressive than even the writers had been able to imagine.

Since he had never illustrated for the general fiction magazines, he made no effort to conventionalize his covers according to the patterns of fiction. (Gernsback also had no experience in the editing of fiction for general circulation, so he had none of the accepted ideas of what covers must be to impose on Paul.)

Paul did, however, have an excellent understanding of the need to make his covers suggest stories to the readers for whom the magazine was meant. He read the stories carefully, with an eye for technical detail and a quick sense of a scene that would make a dramatic cover. He wasn't necessarily looking for the human conflict, but for the situation that was suggestive of future wonder.

Paul has often been accused of being unable to draw human figures and faces well, and most of his science-fiction illustrations—whether covers or interior black-and-whites, which he also did for the magazines—seem to bear this out. His human beings appear to be all alike. The clothes of the men are often right from the popular idea of what an engineer in the field might wear, from boots to bush jackets. Yet I have seen a few later paintings by Paul that show considerable skill at portraiture; and in some of the covers (as in the August 1929 *Science Wonder Stories* cover reproduced in this book), the human heads were no more stylized than the ones on many other magazine covers of the day. Generally, he did not make any great effort to do careful portraits of people—that was not the center of interest for the readers. The machinery and backgrounds, which *were* the center of interest, were executed with great care and skill and with a surprising variety of imagination.

During science fiction's first two decades, Frank R. Paul clearly dominated the field. He set the general style, which most other artists were happy to follow. And he executed far more cover paintings than any other artist could hope to equal. When Hugo Gernsback gave up *Amazing Stories*, Paul went with him to help start two new magazines—*Air Wonder Stories* and *Science Wonder Stories*; these were later combined into *Wonder Stories*, with *Wonder Stories Quarterly* following as a spin-off in which complete novels could be published.

The readers' enthusiasm for his work was always great. In fact, when the first World Science Fiction Convention met in New York City in 1939, Frank R. Paul was the Guest of Honor chosen, rather than any of the popular authors. This tribute has rarely been given to any artist since.

As late as 1953, when Paul was seventy-three years of age, he did a number of covers for a short-lived magazine published by Gernsback. His work seemed even better than it had been before. Perhaps this was because he had more time to devote to them.

The volume of his work during the first two decades of magazine science fiction was enormous. Paul not only did the covers for the various Gernsback magazines; he also drew the interior illustrations in most cases. For several years, these interiors included portraits of the writers, which, even though frequently redrawn from photographs, indicated how well he could depict faces when it was important. He was also a frequent contributor to other magazines in the field. Hence, much of his work must have been done under extreme pressure to finish on time; but very little seems hurried, and most of it reveals meticulous effort to include even the smallest details.

The first artist to do science-fiction covers after Paul was Leo Morey. *Amazing Stories* had passed to new ownership late in 1929, and to the editorship of T. O'Conner Sloan, an octogenarian who had previously been the managing editor. As far as possible, Dr. Sloan attempted to continue the fiction policies of Gernsback; but the services of Paul for covers were no longer available. Probably wisely, Leo Morey made no effort to follow the style of Paul. His covers tended to emphasize the human element much more.

In time, Morey also developed a following among the readers, though not nearly as enthusiastic a one. He did a few fine covers, but he was severely handicapped by the limitations resulting from the way the magazine was then being printed. Only three colors were used, and the absence of the black plate robbed the covers of any depth and sparkle. Additionally, even when freshly printed, most of the covers appeared faded or washed out, as if the inks used in printing had been diluted.

Furthermore, the rates paid for each cover painting were ridiculously low, even for the time. Morey was a commercial artist who could hardly afford to do his most careful work for the pittance he was paid. (Writers fared no better; an author might consider himself lucky to receive $200 for a complete, book-length novel—and then he might have to wait months after the story had been published before he received his check.)

At first, it seemed that the Depression of the 30's would have no effect on science-fiction magazines. The more issues that appeared on the stands, the better they all seemed to sell. In fact, the sales record was so good that Clayton Publications, a major magazine chain, decided to enter the science-fiction market with a third magazine, named *Astounding Stories of Super Science*, in 1930. Despite the imposing title, this magazine was not primarily interested in gadgets and science, as the previous ones had been. Here was a straight pulp adventure magazine, with the emphasis on fast-moving plots and only enough "science" to provide exotic backgrounds for the action. In the stories, men took fifth-dimension tubes to alien worlds, or alien races invaded and enslaved Earth, which was then saved only by the efforts of the hero. And on Mars, the evil Dr. Ku Sui plotted to overthrow the planetary governments; he was constantly being thwarted by Hawk Carse, but always escaped for another episode.

But as the Depression deepened, trouble began for the magazines. Clayton Publications failed in 1933. (That was a sad blow to the writers, who had been getting prompt payment and good rates from *Astounding* for the first time in the history of science fiction.)

At about the same time, *Amazing* and *Wonder* changed to a new and smaller size. (*Wonder* had experimented briefly with this size before.) Previously, the magazines had been just about the size of normal typing paper, 8½ by 11 inches. This had made for attractive covers with plenty of room for the type needed to list the contents. The smaller size—7 by 10 inches, the regular pulp-magazines size of the time—made good composition and full detail much more difficult for the artist.

Then, in 1935, both *Wonder* and *Amazing* began skipping issues, finally going bimonthly. They had already dropped their big quarterlies, which had appeared in addition to the regular publications. And rumors spread throughout science-fiction-fan circles that they were shortly to cease publication altogether.

Wonder Stories did cease publication, but soon reappeared. The magazine had been sold to the Standard Magazine line of Better Publications, which put out a large number of category magazines under the "Thrilling" title. Hence, the new issues were then entitled *Thrilling Wonder Stories*, which seems a little redundant. There was more than a change of title, however; the entire character of the magazine was altered. From then on, far more emphasis was placed on action and adventure, with less attention to engineering and science, than had been true even in *Astounding*

Stories. And the covers, too, underwent a complete transformation.

The Thrilling group of magazines believed in simple market rules, one of which held that a beautiful girl without too many clothes could not hurt sales in any category. The publisher also tended to minimize the value of the art and to maximize the importance of story titles and authors, so that often more type than art was to be seen. (A number of later magazines carried these practices a good deal further, however.) There were still some good covers, but they were rarely up to what science-fiction art had been.

At the beginning, *Thrilling Wonder* used a confusing number of artists. But in time, Earle K. Bergey became more and more the regular cover artist. The same was true for *Startling Stories*, a companion magazine to *Thrilling Wonder* launched in 1939 and devoted to longer lead stories and a larger element of fantasy.

In those days, the magazines carried several back pages devoted to letters from the readers. Many of these letters dealt at length with the artwork. The initial reaction to all those "girlie" covers was one of horror. But eventually, the readers seemed to settle down and at least accept the Bergey girls, though some of the younger readers complained that their mothers made them throw the magazines away unless they tore off the covers first.

Actually, there was little to offend in any Bergey girl, however few clothes she wore. Bergey was a good-natured, conscientious professional who delivered exactly what was asked of him, but who always tried to make his work as pleasant and appropriate as he could.

The very nature of such covers featuring girls—often almost without clothing out in space, where the men are forced to wear full spacesuits—makes most of them rather less than impressive as examples of art. Still, the history of science-fiction art would be incomplete without a few examples. The Winter 1946 *Startling Stories* cover is one of the better examples, with the added interest that it predicts the use of small hand-held rockets for movement in space; much cruder hand-held devices were later used by the astronauts during their space walks.

To the surprise of many of the readers, *Amazing Stories* managed to survive until 1938, when it was sold to the Ziff-Davis Publishing Company, then located in Chicago. This change in location meant that there would have to to be a change in artists, since an art department must be in direct contact with the artists who draw the covers.

The first cover for the magazine under its new management was an experiment in using photography; it showed a masked man holding a girl and seemingly stepping into some vague spaceship in the background. It proved to be pretty disastrous. Science-fiction stories are somehow beyond the normality of photographs. An artist can catch the dream shaped by the writer, but models aren't that versatile.

The third cover was by Robert Fuqua, who did a great many covers for the magazine during the coming years; and many of his covers return in some degree to the type of art that had originally appealed to the readers. Fuqua could draw an interesting machine, and he knew how to compose a picture that would not be lost under all the lettering on the cover.

Amazing Stories, however, was now appealing to a quite different audience than the one it had been slanted toward originally. The stories were often crude and frequently violent, with only the faintest concession to scientific accuracy. I've been told that Ray Palmer, the editor at the time, used to advise his writers that when a story lost action, they should drop an anvil out of the sky; obviously, he meant that figuratively, but some of the stories seemed to use the trick almost literally.

During World War II, the magazines began a trend toward some measure of occultism with the appearance of stories by Richard Shaver. These were based on the idea that there was a race of "deros" living far down under the Earth and influencing men toward evil by means of certain "rays." There was a lot more to the so-called Shaver Mystery, but all of it was essentially occult in its main appeal. The regular science-fiction fans dropped the magazine in shocked disgust, and they were more than replaced by a different type of reader. Inevitably, the change in the character of the magazine had an influence on the type of covers used, and there was little real science-fiction art to be found on *Amazing Stories* for several years.

Before that, however, in 1938 *Amazing* began an interesting publishing experiment of using illustrations on the back covers instead of advertisements. In 1940, Palmer commissioned Frank R. Paul to draw several series of paintings depicting life on other worlds, the cities on those worlds, and similar exotic landscapes. For these, Paul supplied both the background and the drawing, and the result was often enormously interesting. In these illustrations Paul deliberately dropped his interest in machinery and began to render alien landscapes with more detail and imagination than he had previously shown. These paintings were extremely popular with the readers.

Astounding Stories, which had seemed to die with the March 1933 issue, also found a new home. It was purchased by Street & Smith Publications—one of the oldest and strongest of the magazine chains—and was back on the stands with the October 1933 issue. But the result of the change seemed unhappy with the first three issues, which were more weird than science fictional. Then suddenly, with the first issue of 1934, the magazine seemed to take on a new lease. Within a few months it became the leading magazine in the field, a place it has held ever since. There were times when some other magazine managed a larger circulation, but never equal prestige.

The stories rapidly developed a blend of science and much better writing than had previously been found. F. Orlin Tremaine was an experienced editor of high-class pulp magazines. He knew nothing about science fiction at first, but he quickly learned about the field and came to love it; he even wrote a number of stories under various pen names, some of which were acclaimed by the readers.

For several years, most of the cover art was done by Howard V. Brown, and some of these paintings are outstanding examples of science-fiction illustrating. He was extremely versatile, able to draw machinery that was attractive and functional, depict human beings with real character, and show alien forms that were truly alien and yet somehow attractive. I consider his June 1936 cover, illustrating a novel by H. P. Lovecraft, to be one of the best paintings of aliens of all time; and, like most of his paintings, it fits the story it illustrates.

Tremaine's influence on science fiction and its art made for considerable improvement in the field. But a still greater improvement in the fiction came when John W. Campbell replaced him as editor in 1938. Campbell had long been one of the leading writers in the field; his first story appeared in 1930, when he was still in college. He was noted particularly for his stories of "hard science"—stories with an emphasis on the science of physics and on engineering developments. Brown's December 1934 cover illustrates one of Campbell's novels, in which men invent a new method of driving a spaceship and a new source of power by tapping the sun's energy. They then break out of our space into another space, where men are fighting devilish creatures (literally). In winning the war, they hollow out a moon, equip it with fantastic machinery, and drive it through space to destroy the enemy world. It's hard science with a vengeance.

Campbell had another side, however. Under the pseudonym of Don A. Stuart, he had been writing stories with mood and a literary quality unusual for the time. Hence, as an editor, he brought a keen understanding of science plus a strong interest in better writing to the magazine. He passed on much of his skill to the regular writers and also discovered many new writers. Most of the major authors of science fiction today are men he developed, and modern science fiction (as opposed to the old, mechanistic type) is usually dated from Campbell's early days as an editor.

Strangely, however, the covers on the magazine did not show any particular emphasis on science or engineering. Fewer interesting machines appeared on the covers during his editorship than before, and the ones shown were almost too smoothly curved; engineering had to give way to esthetics, apparently. Whether this was Campbell's influence or not is hard to say; he had an art director, but he also made his preferences clearly felt at times.

The one area of science that was given major attention on the covers was that of astronomy. A number of astronomical scenes appeared, many by Chesley Bonestell. Some of these were marvelous as art, but they have appeared many times elsewhere; and they have since been somewhat overshadowed by the real pictures taken in space.

Hubert Rogers did the majority of the covers while Campbell was editor, until the war interrupted his work. He did a few space scenes, but his ships were smoothed until they seemed to be made of modeling clay rather than metal. They were pretty, but hardly convincing—at least from our present knowledge of actual space hardware. Many of his covers emphasized people, so when the story selected for illustrating made them interesting enough, Rogers produced some memorable covers. The merman-human and the girl on the July 1940 *Astounding Science Fiction* (as the magazine was by then titled) are a good example of this. Rogers was also strong on idealized backgrounds, as in the May 1947 cover, drawn after his return from the war.

For several years after the war, the covers for *Astounding* generally tended to become increasingly symbolic. Many made no attempt to illustrate the contents, but were the artist's symbolic representations of, for example, man's attempt to control the atom—and in a few cases, such symbolism was unclear in its meaning. Even when a story *was* illustrated, some of the covers were hardly the detailed, exact depiction that readers had so long accepted. Many of the older readers objected, though some of the younger ones were happy with the change. One such cover was that for December 1947, showing a robot and a dog. Here the artist used the elements of the story he was illustrating, though the cover hardly depicts a particular scene. It's one of the few successful examples of this type of cover.

In a way, Van Dongen's October 1951 cover also symbolizes the story featured; but in this case, though the alien is shown with the world merely symbolized, he is so splendidly drawn and fits the description in the story so well that even the most hardened realist among readers was delighted with it.

Frank Kelly Freas began illustrating for *Astounding* near the end of this symbolic period. His two covers (October 1953 and September 1954) symbolize the stories in the issues—but they do so with graphically science-fictional figures. Freas, incidentally, has gone on to become the most popular illustrator for the science-fiction magazines and paperback books today. Some of his work uses touches of symbolism, but much is strictly representational.

While *Astounding* was straying from the older traditions, *Startling Stories* began returning to them, abandoning their "girlie" formula. The three Schomburg illustrations show scenes in space; machines dominate the pictures.

Science fiction has existed as a separate category of fiction for almost half a century, and the magazine covers reproduced in this book span slightly more than the first half of that period. These were the years when science-fiction art meant art on the covers of the magazines. From 1954 on, the paperback books began to dominate the field, and the story of that art is another tale for another day.

All the covers in this volume are taken from the major magazines of that early period: *Amazing Stories*, *Air-Science-Thrilling Wonder Stories* (and its sister publication, *Startling Stories*) and *Astounding Stories-Science Fiction*. In one form or another, each of these three publications (counting *Startling* and *Wonder* as one) managed to exist for more than twenty years. *Amazing* and *Astounding* (now renamed *Analog Science Fact/ Science Fiction*) are still being published, though *Wonder* and *Startling* were discontinued in 1955.

There were many other magazines during the period, but most of the cover art they carried was of questionable interest. *Galaxy* and *Fantasy & Science Fiction* were just then becoming established, so their influence was strongest in later years.

The covers reproduced here are arranged chronologically as the best way to demonstrate the development of science-fiction art. They represent the best of what caught the attention and drew the readers to the magazines, and they tell a good deal about the real science fiction of the period.

They do *not*, however, conform to many of the cliché ideas some people have of the magazines. Mention science fiction and most of those who don't read it think of bug-eyed monsters and little green men—or of that "Buck Rogers stuff." Well, I've included one bug-eyed monster—an enormous fly, and it had to be "bug-eyed," since it *is* an insect. And there's one little green man staring out of a keyhole. But he isn't the little green man one might expect to come from a flying saucer.

As for "Buck Rogers stuff," there's nothing particularly cartoonlike about most of the art. Anyhow, Buck Rogers was really science-fiction stuff. The comic strip was created from a story by Phil Nowlan that first appeared in *Amazing Stories* in 1928 entitled "Armageddon 2419." It was a better-than-average story for its day, but hardly representative of later science fiction.

Flying saucers were around early on science-fiction covers, however. Paul's November 1929 *Science Wonder Stories* cover shows a fine picture of a disk-shaped ship flying through space. Most of the early ships of science fiction were circular or globular, and the classic cigar shape came much later. Sometimes one might wonder whether those drawings of Paul were perhaps responsible for the shape of UFO ships described by the Ufologists.

Many of the themes depicted on those early covers are also interesting in their prediction of things to come. The problem of energy shortages was accurately predicted in many stories, and one possible solution is shown on the August 1929 *Science Wonder Stories*, which illustrates a giant mirror in space, designed to catch the energy from the sun and beam its power back to Earth. (This could also be a frightening weapon if misused.)

Spacesuits were already well developed by the artists. The August 1931 *Amazing Stories* cover shows two men in suits floating in space. The design isn't precisely that used by NASA, but it is very close. The chief error is in the color, which should have been white to reflect the heat of the sun. But the color of all spacesuits shown was chosen for its artistic value, of course, though quite a few stories did mention white as being desirable.

Mutations and the ability of man to alter his genetic pattern were familiar themes long before the atomic bomb or the discovery of DNA. The two altered humans on the cover of the July 1940 *Astounding Science Fiction* are people who have been changed to enable them to live in the oceans. And the reason for this? A need for the increasing population of Earth to discover more room and more sources of food than could be found on land.

Some violence is shown on these old covers, but less than could be found in almost any other group of magazines of the period, and far less than is shown regularly on television. Comparatively few stories of science fiction went in for direct, personal violence. Even most of the wars between aliens and humans were rather impersonal, with little contact violence depicted. This does not excuse the amount of such warfare encountered in science fiction during its early days; perhaps war was treated far too casually. But, compared with the many magazines devoted directly to aerial combat and other kinds of war, science fiction was rather peaceable for its time. And the covers showed less of such war violence than the stories told.

Generally, science fiction is considered to be rather lacking in humor. Perhaps there is rather less humor than there might be, but even these covers show some evidence of it. There's the little green Martian staring through the keyhole. And, to me, the machine on the September 1929 *Science Wonder Stories* cover has always had a strong element of humor.

One of the basic themes of science fiction during the early years was man's desire to get out into space. It was taken for granted that someday men would ride rockets to the moon and eventually beyond to the planets. At the time, many scientists were sure that it could not be done. Even as late as 1956, people explained to me that rockets couldn't work in space, because there was no air to push against! The major error in the predictions of science fiction was the date—most writers seemed to assume space travel would come no earlier than 2000.

The covers reflect that interest in space, since ten of the first twenty—during the first ten years of science fiction—show scenes in space.

But just as the writers were wrong about the date, the artists were wrong in depicting Earth as seen from space. They show Earth as if it were possible to view the seas and continents clearly, without any real blanket of clouds to obscure the view. Now, having taken pictures of Earth from satellites and from the moon, we know that it's often difficult to distinguish the outlines of the continents, much less to see finer details.

But generally, these pictures of space are as fascinating now as when they were drawn. And the fact that we actually got out beyond Earth to see the reality of space can partly be blamed on the covers and the stories that inspired men to keep trying. Most of those who pioneered our way into space were men who had read and shared the dreams of science fiction when they were young.

There has never been any other form of magazine art with quite the impact of that on the old science-fiction covers. Many of the magazines are decaying today, making restoration of the original art difficult. But in going through hundreds of such magazines to select these covers, I found that the imagination and the wonder had not faded in the slightest with time.

LESTER DEL REY

FANTASTIC SCIENCE-FICTION ART 1926-1954

EDITED WITH AN INTRODUCTION BY LESTER DEL REY